THE JPS B'NAI MITZVAH TORAH COMMENTARY

Ha'azinu (Deuteronomy 32:1–52)
Haftarah (2 Samuel 22:1–51)

Rabbi Jeffrey K. Salkin

The Jewish Publication Society · Philadelphia
University of Nebraska Press · Lincoln

INTRODUCTION

News flash: the most important thing about becoming bar or bat mitzvah isn't the party. Nor is it the presents. Nor even being able to celebrate with your family and friends—as wonderful as those things are. Nor is it even standing before the congregation and reading the prayers of the liturgy—as important as that is.

No, the most important thing about becoming bar or bat mitzvah is sharing Torah with the congregation. And why is that? Because of all Jewish skills, that is the most important one.

Here is what is true about rites of passage: you can tell what a culture values by the tasks it asks its young people to perform on their way to maturity. In American culture, you become responsible for driving, responsible for voting, and yes, responsible for drinking responsibly.

In some cultures, the rite of passage toward maturity includes some kind of trial, or a test of strength. Sometimes, it is a kind of "outward bound" camping adventure. Among the Maasai tribe in Africa, it is traditional for a young person to hunt and kill a lion. In some Hispanic cultures, fifteen year-old girls celebrate the *quinceañera*, which marks their entrance into maturity.

What is Judaism's way of marking maturity? It combines both of these rites of passage: *responsibility* and *test*. You show that you are on your way to becoming a *responsible* Jewish adult through a public *test* of strength and knowledge—reading or chanting Torah, and then teaching it to the congregation.

This is the most important Jewish ritual mitzvah (commandment), and that is how you demonstrate that you are, truly, bar or bat mitzvah—old enough to be responsible for the mitzvot.

What Is Torah?

So, what exactly is the Torah? You probably know this already, but let's review.

The Torah (teaching) consists of "the five books of Moses," sometimes also called the *chumash* (from the Hebrew word *chameish,* which means "five"), or, sometimes, the Greek word Pentateuch (which means "the five teachings").

Here are the five books of the Torah, with their common names and their Hebrew names.

> - **Genesis (The beginning), which in Hebrew is Bere'shit (from the first words—"When God began to create").** Bere'shit spans the years from Creation to Joseph's death in Egypt. Many of the Bible's best stories are in Genesis: the creation story itself; Adam and Eve in the Garden of Eden; Cain and Abel; Noah and the Flood; and the tales of the Patriarchs and Matriarchs, Abraham, Isaac, Jacob, Sarah, Rebekah, Rachel, and Leah. It also includes one of the greatest pieces of world literature, the story of Joseph, which is actually the oldest complete novel in history, comprising more than one-quarter of all Genesis.
> - **Exodus (Getting out), which in Hebrew is Shemot (These are the names).** Exodus begins with the story of the Israelite slavery in Egypt. It then moves to the rise of Moses as a leader, and the Israelites' liberation from slavery. After the Israelites leave Egypt, they experience the miracle of the parting of the Sea of Reeds (or "Red Sea"); the giving of the Ten Commandments at Mount Sinai; the idolatry of the Golden Calf; and the design and construction of the Tabernacle and of the ark for the original tablets of the law, which our ancestors carried with them in the desert. Exodus also includes various ethical and civil laws, such as "You shall not wrong a stranger or oppress him, for you were strangers in the land of Egypt" (22:20).
> - **Leviticus (about the Levites), or, in Hebrew, Va-yikra' (And God called).** It goes into great detail about the kinds of sacrifices that the ancient Israelites brought as offerings; the laws of ritual purity; the animals that were permitted and forbidden for eating (the beginnings of the tradition of kashrut, the Jewish dietary laws); the diagnosis of various skin diseases; the ethical laws of holiness; the ritual calendar of the Jewish year; and various agricultural laws concerning the treatment of the Land of Israel. Leviticus is basically the manual of ancient Judaism.

> **Numbers (because the book begins with the census of the Isra-elites), or, in Hebrew, Be-midbar (In the wilderness).** The book describes the forty years of wandering in the wilderness and the various rebellions against Moses. The constant theme: "Egypt wasn't so bad. Maybe we should go back." The greatest rebellion against Moses was the negative reports of the spies about the Land of Israel, which discouraged the Israelites from wanting to move forward into the land. For that reason, the "wilderness gen-eration" must die off before a new generation can come into ma-turity and finish the journey.

> **Deuteronomy (The repetition of the laws of the Torah), or, in Hebrew, Devarim (The words).** The final book of the Torah is, essentially, Moses's farewell address to the Israelites as they pre-pare to enter the Land of Israel. Here we find various laws that had been previously taught, though sometimes with different wording. Much of Deuteronomy contains laws that will be im-portant to the Israelites as they enter the Land of Israel—laws concerning the establishment of a monarchy and the ethics of warfare. Perhaps the most famous passage from Deuteronomy contains the *Shema,* the declaration of God's unity and unique-ness, and the *Ve-ahavta,* which follows it. Deuteronomy ends with the death of Moses on Mount Nebo as he looks across the Jordan Valley into the land that he will not enter.

Jews read the Torah in sequence—starting with Bere'shit right af-ter Simchat Torah in the autumn, and then finishing Devarim on the following Simchat Torah. Each Torah portion is called a parashah (di-vision; sometimes called a *sidrah,* a place in the order of the Torah reading). The stories go around in a full circle, reminding us that we can always gain more insights and more wisdom from the Torah. This means that if you don't "get" the meaning this year, don't worry—it will come around again.

And What Else? The Haftarah

We read or chant the Torah from the Torah scroll—the most sacred thing that a Jewish community has in its possession. The Torah is written without vowels, and the ability to read it and chant it is part of the challenge and the test.

But there is more to the synagogue reading. Every Torah reading has an accompanying haftarah reading. Haftarah means "conclusion," because there was once a time when the service actually ended with that reading. Some scholars believe that the reading of the haftarah originated at a time when non-Jewish authorities outlawed the reading of the Torah, and the Jews read the haftarah sections instead. In fact, in some synagogues, young people who become bar or bat mitzvah read very little Torah and instead read the entire haftarah portion.

The haftarah portion comes from the Nevi'im, the prophetic books, which are the second part of the Jewish Bible. It is either read or chanted from a Hebrew Bible, or maybe from a booklet or a photocopy.

The ancient sages chose the haftarah passages because their themes reminded them of the words or stories in the Torah text. Sometimes, they chose *haftarah* with special themes in honor of a festival or an upcoming festival.

Not all books in the prophetic section of the Hebrew Bible consist of prophecy. Several are historical. For example:

The book of Joshua tells the story of the conquest and settlement of Israel.

The book of Judges speaks of the period of early tribal rulers who would rise to power, usually for the purpose of uniting the tribes in war against their enemies. Some of these leaders are famous: Deborah, the great prophetess and military leader, and Samson, the biblical strong man.

The books of Samuel start with Samuel, the last judge, and then move to the creation of the Israelite monarchy under Saul and David (approximately 1000 BCE).

The books of Kings tell of the death of King David, the rise of King Solomon, and how the Israelite kingdom split into the Northern Kingdom of Israel and the Southern Kingdom of Judah (approximately 900 BCE).

And then there are the books of the prophets, those spokesmen for God whose words fired the Jewish conscience. Their names are immortal: Isaiah, Jeremiah, Ezekiel, Amos, Hosea, among others.

Someone once said: "There is no evidence of a biblical prophet ever being invited back a second time for dinner." Why? Because the prophets were tough. They had no patience for injustice, apathy, or hypocrisy. No one escaped their criticisms. Here's what they taught:

> God commands the Jews to behave decently toward one another. In fact, God cares more about basic ethics and decency than about ritual behavior.
> God chose the Jews *not* for special privileges, but for special duties to humanity.
> As bad as the Jews sometimes were, there was always the possibility that they would improve their behavior.
> As bad as things might be now, it will not always be that way. Someday, there will be universal justice and peace. Human history is moving forward toward an ultimate conclusion that some call the Messianic Age: a time of universal peace and prosperity for the Jewish people and for all the people of the world.

Your Mission—To Teach Torah to the Congregation

On the day when you become bar or bat mitzvah, you will be reading, or chanting, Torah—in Hebrew. You will be reading, or chanting, the haftarah—in Hebrew. That is the major skill that publicly marks the becoming of bar or bat mitzvah. But, perhaps even more important than that, you need to be able to teach something about the Torah portion, and perhaps the haftarah as well.

And that is where this book comes in. It will be a very valuable resource for you, and your family, in the b'nai mitzvah process.

Here is what you will find in it:

> A brief **summary** of every Torah portion. This is a basic overview of the portion; and, while it might not refer to everything in the Torah portion, it will explain its most important aspects.
> A list of the **major ideas** in the Torah portion. The purpose: to make the Torah portion real, in ways that we can relate to. Every Torah portion contains unique ideas, and when you put all

of those ideas together, you actually come up with a list of Judaism's most important ideas.

› Two *divrei Torah* ("words of Torah," or "sermonettes") for each portion. These *divrei Torah* explain significant aspects of the Torah portion in accessible, reader-friendly language. Each *devar Torah* contains references to **traditional** Jewish sources (those that were written before the modern era), as well as **modern** sources and quotes. We have searched, far and wide, to find sources that are unusual, interesting, and not just the "same old stuff" that many people already know about the Torah portion. Why did we include these minisermons in the volume? Not because we want you to simply copy those sermons and pass them off as your own (that would be cheating), though you are free to quote from them. We included them so that you can see what is possible— how you can try to make meaning for yourself out of the words of Torah.

› **Connections:** This is perhaps the most valuable part. It's a list of questions that you can ask yourself, or that others might help you think about—any of which can lead to the creation of your *devar Torah.*

Note: you don't have to like everything that's in a particular Torah portion. Some aren't that loveable. Some are hard to understand; some are about religious practices that people today might find confusing, and even offensive; some contain ideas that we might find totally outmoded.

But this doesn't have to get in the way. After all, most kids spend a lot of time thinking about stories that contain ideas that modern people would find totally bizarre. Any good medieval fantasy story falls into that category.

And we also believe that, if you spend just a little bit of time with those texts, you can begin to understand what the author was trying to say.

This volume goes one step further. Sometimes, the haftarah comes off as a second thought, and no one really thinks about it. We have tried to solve that problem by including a **summary** of each haftarah, and then a mini-sermon on the haftarah. This will help you learn how these sacred words are relevant to today's world, and even to your own life.

All Bible quotations come from the NJPS translation, which is found in the many different editions of the JPS TANAKH; in the Conservative movement's *Etz Hayim: Torah and Commentary;* in the Reform movement's *Torah: A Modern Commentary;* and in other Bible commentaries and study guides.

How Do I Write a *Devar Torah?*

It really is easier than it looks.

There are many ways of thinking about the *devar Torah.* It is, of course, a short sermon on the meaning of the Torah (and, perhaps, the haftarah) portion. It might even be helpful to think of the *devar Torah* as a "book report" on the portion itself.

The most important thing you can know about this sacred task is: *Learn* the words. *Love* the words. Teach people what it could mean to *live* the words.

Here's a basic outline for a *devar Torah:*

"My Torah portion is (name of portion) _____,
   from the book of _____, chapter

   _____.

"In my Torah portion, we learn that_____
   (Summary of portion)

"For me, the most important lesson of this Torah portion is (what
   is the best thing in the portion? Take the portion as a whole;
   your *devar Torah* does not have to be only, or specifically, on the
   verses that you are reading).

"As I learned my Torah portion, I found myself wondering:
   ➤ *Raise a question that the Torah portion itself raises.*
   ➤ *"Pick a fight"* with the portion. Argue with it.
   ➤ *Answer a question* that is listed in the "Connections" section of
     each Torah portion.
   ➤ *Suggest a question to your rabbi* that you would want the rabbi
     to answer in his or her own *devar Torah* or sermon.

"I have lived the values of the Torah by _____
(here, you can talk about how the Torah portion relates to your
own life. If you have done a mitzvah project, you can talk about
that here).

How To Keep It from Being Boring
(and You from Being Bored)

Some people just don't like giving traditional speeches. From our per-
spective, that's really okay. Perhaps you can teach Torah in a different
way—one that makes sense to you.

> Write an "open letter" to one of the characters in your Torah por-
  tion. "Dear Abraham: I hope that your trip to Canaan was not too
  hard . . ." "Dear Moses: Were you afraid when you got the Ten
  Commandments on Mount Sinai? I sure would have been . . ."
> Write a news story about what happens. Imagine yourself to
  be a television or news reporter. "Residents of neighboring cities were horrified yesterday as the wicked cities of Sodom and
  Gomorrah were burned to the ground. Some say that God was
  responsible . . ."
> Write an imaginary interview with a character in your Torah portion.
> Tell the story from the point of view of another character, or a mi-
  nor character, in the story. For instance, tell the story of the Gar-
  den of Eden from the point of view of the serpent. Or the story
  of the Binding of Isaac from the point of view of the ram, which
  was substituted for Isaac as a sacrifice. Or perhaps the story of
  the sale of Joseph from the point of view of his coat, which was
  stripped off him and dipped in a goat's blood.
> Write a poem about your Torah portion.
> Write a song about your Torah portion.
> Write a play about your Torah portion, and have some friends act
  it out with you.
> Create a piece of artwork about your Torah portion.

The bottom line is: Make this a joyful experience. Yes—it could
even be fun.

The Very Last Thing You Need to Know at This Point

The Torah scroll is written without vowels. Why? Don't *sofrim* (Torah scribes) know the vowels?

Of course they do.

So, why do they leave the vowels out?

One reason is that the Torah came into existence at a time when sages were still arguing about the proper vowels, and the proper pronunciation.

But here is another reason: The Torah text, as we have it today, and as it sits in the scroll, is actually *an unfinished work*. Think of it: the words are just sitting there. Because they have no vowels, it is as if they have no voice.

When we read the Torah publicly, we give voice to the ancient words. And when we find meaning in those ancient words, and we talk about those meanings, those words jump to life. They enter our lives. They make our world deeper and better.

Mazal tov to you, and your family. This is your journey toward Jewish maturity. Love it.

THE TORAH

❖ Ha'azinu: Deuteronomy 32:1–52

This Torah portion is essentially a long poem, delivered by Moses, in which he recounts the history of the Jewish people (in a beautiful but quirky way). In it he describes what would happen if and when the People of Israel betray the covenant with God. It contains a number of verses that will be familiar to people who attend services.

The parashah ends with God reminding Moses of his imminent death, and the reason why he will not be able to enter the Land of Israel: he and his brother Aaron broke faith with God at Meribat-Kadesh when Moses disobeyed God and, in an effort to draw forth water from a rock, hit the rock rather than speaking to it. Almost as a "tease," God allows Moses to view the land from a distance but not enter it.

This portion, with its constant reminder of the Jewish people's sins, is usually read on Shabbat Shuvah, the Shabbat of Repentance, which comes between Rosh Hashanah and Yom Kippur.

Summary

› Moses begins by calling on the heavens and the earth to
  ha'azinu—"give ear," listen and pay attention. Moses doesn't really believe that the heavens and the earth can actually hear; his
  calling out this way is an expression of his desire that the entire
  cosmos should know what is going on between God and the Jewish people. (32:1–3)
› Moses calls God *"Ha-Tzur,"* the Rock, and proclaims that God's ac-
  tions are perfect, and that God is never false. If anyone is false, it is
  the Jewish people, who are portrayed as children who rebel against
  their parent, God (the "Father"), who created them. (32:1–6)
› Moses reminds the people that they should ask their parents and
  their elders about the way of the world and that God determined
  the boundaries of all the nations. (32:7–9)
› Moses describes the early history of the Jewish people in a rather
  creative way: as an orphan child found by God in the desert and
  then reared by God. This continues the theme of God as parent.
  (32:10–14)
› Moses describes what God's anger will be like when the People of Israel abandon God and worship false gods. God will pun-
  ish them by unleashing a nation upon them that is as worthless
  as the gods they have worshiped. God will treat the Israelites exactly as God treated the wicked inhabitants of Sodom and Gomorrah. That will be God's way of proving that God is the only
  God. (32:15–43)

The Big Ideas

> **Deuteronomy almost "invents" the idea of listening and hearing.** Well, not quite true, but the various terms for listening and hearing—*shema* and *ha'azinu*—have prominent roles in this final book of the Torah. It is as if Moses is making sure that his words do not go to waste. Hearing and listening do not only mean something that happens with our ears. The best (and perhaps the only) way to listen is to be fully present for another person.

> **One of Judaism's most powerful images of God is of a parent.** The parent-child image of the Jewish relationship with God is one of the most significant features of the High Holy Day season. Sometimes we refer to God as *Avinu* ("our Father" or "our Parent") and sometimes as *Malkheinu* ("our King" or "our Sovereign"), and sometimes, like on the High Holy Days, we merge these two images together. While most people cannot understand what it means to relate to a king or a monarch, it is easy to think about what it means to relate to a parent. Parents love us, but they also discipline us, because they want the best for us. At the same time, we have a duty to honor God, just as we honor our parents—even when it is very hard to do so.

> **Idolatry is the worship of gods and of objects that are worthless.** Notice the way that Moses refers to the false gods that the people will worship: "no-gods" (32:17)—gods that are not even the gods that other nations worship, not really gods at all. Those gods are also referred to as "gods they had never known; new ones, who came but lately." The worst thing about these gods is that they are "new," and not timeless like God.

Divrei Torah

WATCH GOD MORPH

Do you ever think about God? Maybe; maybe not. A lot of people don't, or, when they do, they get very confused. That's because the first question they are likely to ask is: Who (or what) is God?

The problem is not that we don't have enough ways to think about God. Rather, it's the opposite—we might actually have too many. Just look at the way that God is portrayed in this Torah portion. First, God is described as a rock. Then, a few verses later, God is portrayed as a father—but a father who just happens to find the Jewish people in the desert, like homeless infants, and adopts them. But wait: God becomes a mother eagle. And then God is like a human mother who nurses her young. Verses later God is like a warrior.

Please stop, you are probably saying. Can't the biblical author simply make up his or her mind? What is God, anyway?

And it's not as if these are the only images of God that we have. This Torah portion is read between Rosh Hashanah and Yom Kippur, when we call God Father and King, and we imagine our relationship to God as sheep to their shepherd, or grapes to the vine keeper. As the *machzor* (High Holy Day prayer book) puts it: "For we are Your people, and You are our father. We are your flock of sheep, and You are our keeper. We are Your vineyard, and You are our vintner."

This is fine if you get the agricultural images. But, what if you never saw a sheep in your life? What if you have never seen a vineyard, and the only grapes you know are the ones that you buy at the grocery store?

Professor Rachel Adler teaches: "God is imaged in rapid succession as a rock, father, a mother eagle, a birth giver, and a warrior. As long as we are simply receptive and allow the diverse images to flow past, we experience no contradictions. But when we stop the flow and try to reconcile the images logically, we run into trouble." In other words, when it comes to talking about God, don't look for consistency. It's not going to happen.

Talking about God is not easy. After all, when Moses first encounters God, Moses asks him: "When the Jews ask me who sent you, what name shall I give them?" God replies, *"Ehyeh asher ehyeh."* Some people like to translate that as "I am what I am." This makes God more than a little arrogant: "You don't like me? Tough." More than that: to say that God is what God is makes the whole notion of God very static and very present tense. "What you see [well, not really] is what you get." And remember: the word *ehyeh* is clearly the future tense for "to be." *Ehyeh* means, in effect, "I will be." God's "future" is unfinished. God is, as they say, a work in progress. And if God is not "done" yet, then neither are we.

THE NEW ISN'T ALWAYS BETTER

Let me guarantee you something, right now. You are going to be getting gifts when you celebrate becoming bar or bat mitzvah. You may be getting money and clothing and, basically, a lot of "stuff." Much of that "stuff," especially if it includes electronics and computer stuff, will be the newest, the best, and the fastest.

Sure. Until something newer, better, and faster comes out.

So, if you don't know already, then it's time you learn about the way the world works. Much of what goes on is based on the fact that you're a consumer. You, and everyone else you know, buy things. But we not only buy things, we "consume" them. "Consume" means to use it up—as in "consuming" resources. The basic idea here is that once we have used something and it is no longer usable we have consumed it—and then we throw it away, waiting for the next great thing to come along. If you don't believe this, check out electronics stores that allow people to donate old cell phones, and music players, and televisions. Last year's model? Who needs it? Even last month's model might be too old.

So, let's go back to the Torah portion. The worst thing that Moses can say about the false gods that the Israelites will no doubt worship is that they are "new ones, who came but lately, who stirred not your fathers' fears" (32:17). There are at least a hundred names for God in Judaism. One of them is the Aramaic term *atika kaddisha*, "the Holy Ancient One," which appears in the biblical book of Daniel. A god—or, at the very least, the Jewish God—should be as old as creation itself.

Our stuff always seems to need an upgrade. But God doesn't need an upgrade (maybe the way we talk about God needs the upgrade, but that's a different story).

How can we focus less on our "stuff"? Take Shabbat. Traditional Jews don't shop on Shabbat because Jewish law forbids the handling of money on the Sabbath. But there is a deeper reason: one day a week we can think about not what we own and must have, but just about who we are and our relationships. Modern Jewish theologian Abraham Joshua Heschel writes: "In regard to gifts, to outward possessions, we can have them and we should be able to do without them. On the Sabbath, handling money is a desecration, on which man avows his independence of that which is the world's chief idol."

Ultimately, we need to focus less on our "stuff" and more on who we are as human beings. As the ancient sage Ben Zoma writes: "Who is rich? The one who is content with what he has."

Connections

> - In what way is God like a parent? What kind of parent is God?
> - What do you think of all those other images of God? Which one do you like the best?
> - How do you imagine God? How have your ideas about God changed as you've gotten older? In what way is God like a rock?
> - Do you believe that people concentrate too much on their possessions? Can you offer some examples? What are other, more important things for people to be thinking about? How can you make this happen in your own life?

THE HAFTARAH

❖ Ha'azinu: 2 Samuel 22:1–51

The drama of "will we return to Israel?" of the last several *haftarah* is now complete. With the coming of Rosh Hashanah, the Jews are "home"—not only geographically, in the Land of Israel during ancient times, but "home" as well in modern times, now that we have a re-established Jewish state, and have synagogues that build and nurture active Jewish communities.

Knowing this, we can now go back to linking the Torah portion thematically with the haftarah portion. Back to finding common themes and language. This week's Torah portion contains Moses's farewell song to the Jewish people. And this week's haftarah presents the song that King David composed in his old age. So the connection between the two is farewell songs.

What rests heavily upon David's memory? It is the fact that when he was younger, King Saul pursued him and tried to kill him. Saul had been jealous of David's growing popularity, and that jealousy pushed him into a murderous madness. But David is not killed, and he thanks God for having saved him.

As we know, King David is considered one of the Jewish people's most important poets. Jewish lore and tradition credit him with writing many of the psalms in the Bible. And, as a poet, David had no shortage of ways of thinking about God. He compares God to many things, and these different images teach us that our ways of thinking about God are hardly frozen; they can and do change.

Meeting God—On Our Own Terms

Let's imagine King David sitting down and coming up with a list of terms for God. But, before he can do that, he has to think about why he is talking to God in the first place. David is grateful to God, whom he credits with saving him. That's why most of his terms for God are about David's own sense of security.

He calls God a "rock" (22:3), which means that he believes God is sturdy and unchanging. He calls God a "shield" (22:3), reminding us that the six-pointed "Jewish star" is sometimes called a Magen David (Shield of David), because David believes that God has defended him from Saul. He calls God a "stronghold" (22:35)—a fortress. (There is a Christian hymn called "A Mighty Fortress Is Our God.") He calls God a "lamp" (22:29). Perhaps it was because David hid from Saul in caves, which tend to be dark, and thinking about God was like shining a little bit of light into that darkness.

And, for good measure, David throws in some God imagery that was popular in his time—images that we have totally abandoned. "Smoke went up from His nostrils, from His mouth came devouring fire; live coals blazed forth from Him. He bent the sky and came down, thick cloud beneath His feet. He mounted a cherub and flew; he was seen on the wings of the wind" (22:10–11). Yes, there were some ancient Jews who thought that God was like, well, a dragon, but a dragon who could bend the sky and who rode on a cherub, a mythical angel-like figure—whom we have already met, because there were representations of the cherubim over the ark in the ancient Tabernacle.

What can we learn from this? If David was not consistent in his way of experiencing God, that means we do not have to be consistent, either. Think of how we experience God on the High Holy Days:

We are Your people; you are our King.
We are Your children, You are our Father.
We are Your possession; You are our Portion.
We are Your flock; You are our Shepherd.
We are Your vineyard; You are our Keeper.
We are Your friend; you are our Beloved." (*Ki Anu Amekha*)

Many of those ways of understanding the God relationship are familiar, but notice: they go from royal terms, to paternal terms, to agricultural terms, and finally to a deep sense of human relationship and affection.

But, let's admit, we can never fully "get" God. Rabbi Abraham Isaac Kook, the first chief rabbi of prestate Palestine, wrote: "All names and titles of God reveal but a small and dim spark of the hidden light toward which the soul really yearns and to which it calls out."

All that we say and think about God, all that we teach and sing about God, all that we think we know about God—these are all radical understatements. They are only sparks of what we think we know and what we think we want to know. But those sparks are there and if you tend them and if you poke them with a stick, they will flame into a fire.

❖ Notes

CPSIA information can be obtained
at www.ICGtesting.com
Printed in the USA
LVHW090002270319
611895LV00005BA/443/P